Anthology of
CHRISTMAS SONGS

8TH EDITION

ISBN 978-1-4234-9381-5

HAL•LEONARD®
CORPORATION
7777 W. BLUEMOUND RD. P.O. BOX 13819 MILWAUKEE, WI 53213

Visit Hal Leonard Online at
www.halleonard.com

ALL I WANT FOR CHRISTMAS IS YOU

Words and Music by MARIAH CAREY
and WALTER AFANASIEFF

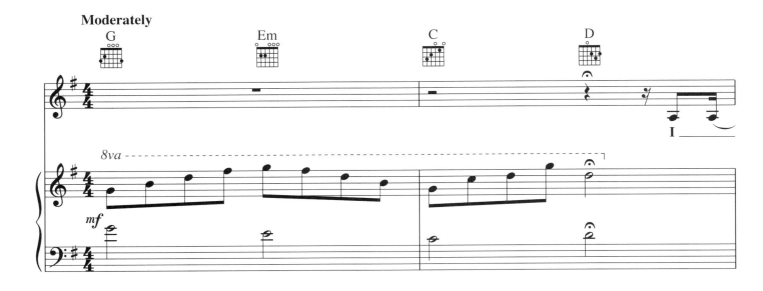

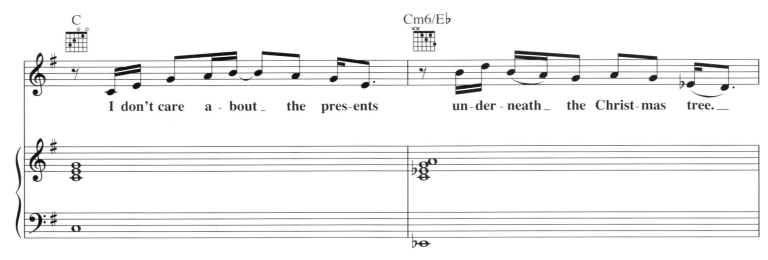

AWAY IN A MANGER

Traditional
Words by JOHN T. McFARLAND (v.3)
Music by JAMES R. MURRAY

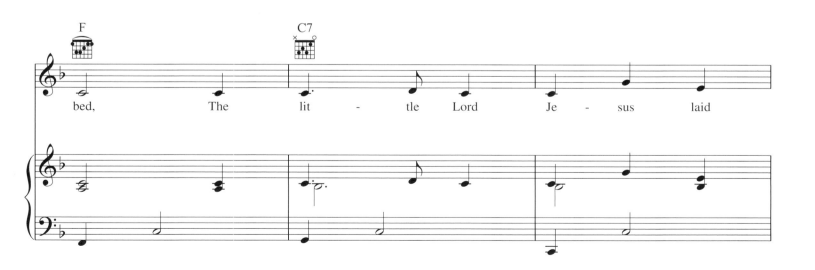

ALMOST DAY

Words and Music by
HUDDIE LEDBETTER

ANGELS WE HAVE HEARD ON HIGH

Traditional French Carol
Translated by JAMES CHADWICK

AULD LANG SYNE

Words by ROBERT BURNS
Traditional Scottish Melody

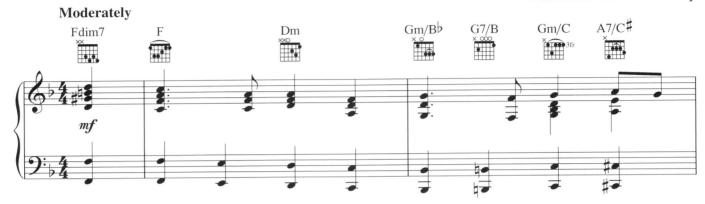

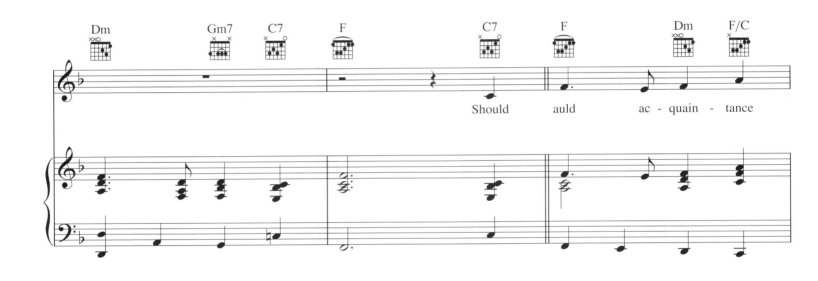

Should auld ac - quain - tance

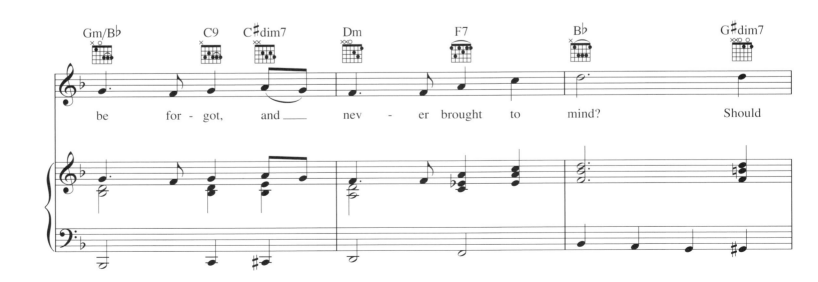

be for - got, and ___ nev - er brought to mind? Should

BECAUSE IT'S CHRISTMAS
(For All the Children)

Music by BARRY MANILOW
Lyric by BRUCE SUSSMAN and JACK FELDMAN

CAROL OF THE BELLS

Ukrainian Christmas Carol

BLUE CHRISTMAS

Words and Music by BILLY HAYES
and JAY JOHNSON

Moderately

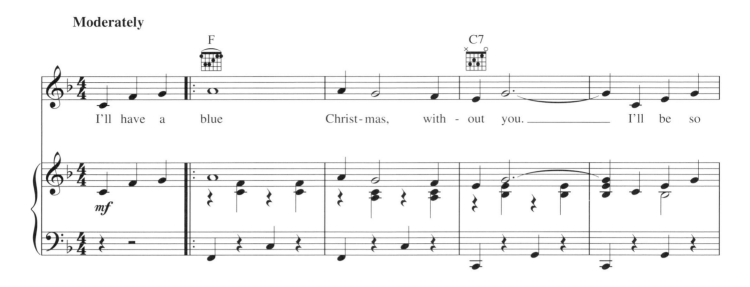

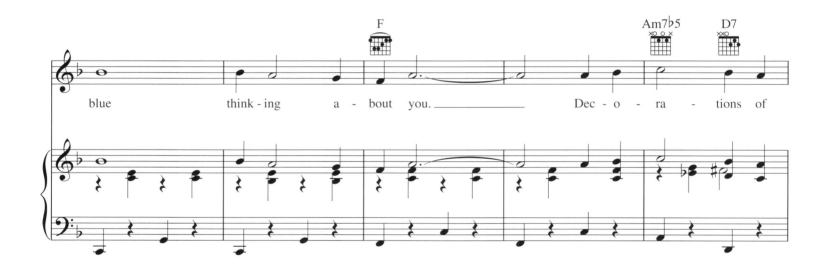

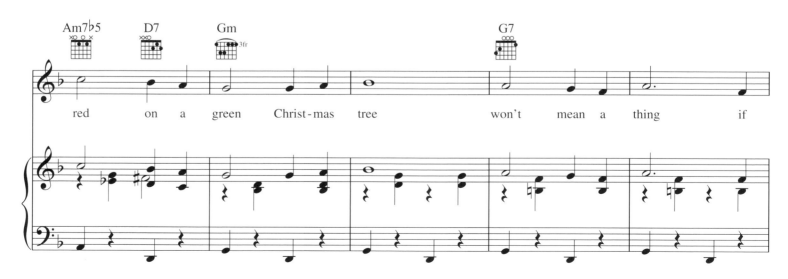

CAROLING, CAROLING

Words by WIHLA HUTSON
Music by ALFRED BURT

CHRIST WAS BORN
ON CHRISTMAS DAY

Traditional

C-H-R-I-S-T-M-A-S

Words by JENNY LOU CARSON
Music by EDDY ARNOLD

CHRISTMAS IS

Lyrics by SPENCE MAXWELL
Music by PERCY FAITH

Christ-mas is sleigh-bells,   Christ-mas is shar-ing,

Christ-mas is hol-ly,   Christ-mas is car-ing.

THE CHRISTMAS SONG
(Chestnuts Roasting on an Open Fire)

Music and Lyric by MEL TORMÉ
and ROBERT WELLS

43

THE CHRISTMAS WALTZ

Words by SAMMY CAHN
Music by JULE STYNE

CHRISTMASTIME

Words and Music by MICHAEL W. SMITH
and JOANNA CARLSON

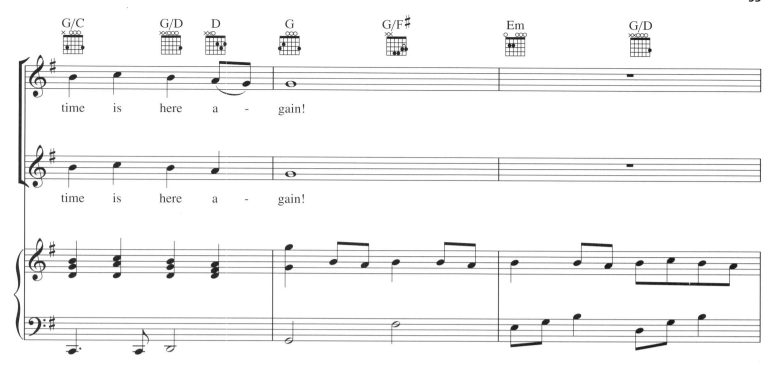

time is here a - gain!

time is here a - gain!

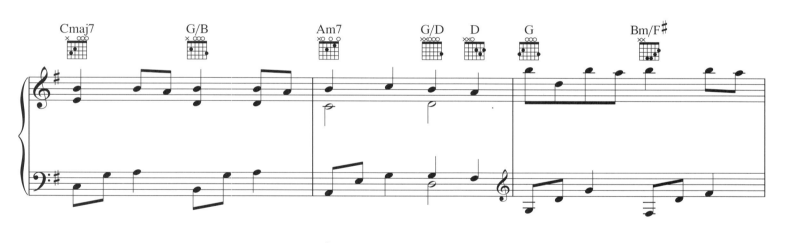

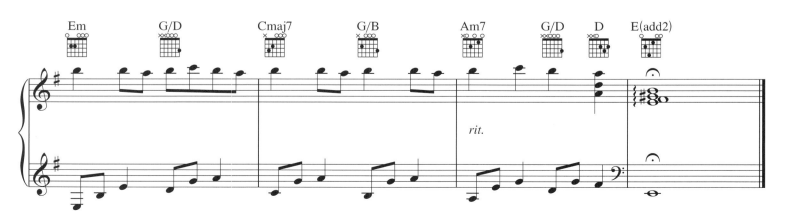

rit.

COLD DECEMBER NIGHTS

Words and Music by MICHAEL McCARY
and SHAWN STOCKMAN

Why aren't _ you next ___ to me _____ cel - e - brat - ing

COVENTRY CAROL

Words by ROBERT CROO
Traditional English Melody

Tenderly

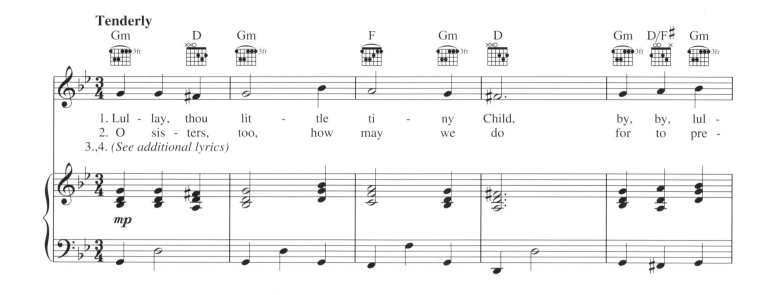

1. Lul - lay, thou lit - tle ti - ny Child, by, by, lul -
2. O sis - ters, too, how may we do for to pre -
3.,4. *(See additional lyrics)*

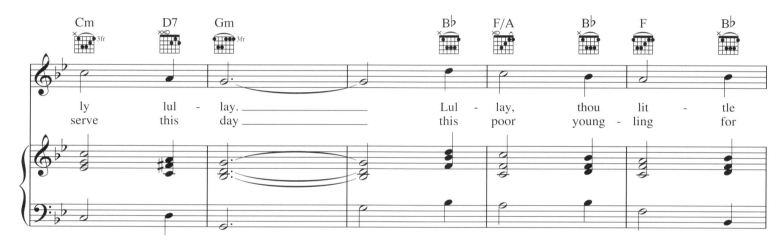

ly lul - lay. _____ Lul - lay, thou lit - tle
serve this day _____ this poor young - ling for

ti - ny Child, by, by, lul - ly lul - lay. _____
whom we sing, by, by, lul - ly lul - lay? _____

Additional Lyrics

3. Herod the king,
   In his raging,
   Charged he hath this day.
   His men of might,
   In his own sight,
   All young children to slay.

4. That woe is me,
   Poor child for thee!
   And ever morn and day,
   For thy parting
   Neither say nor sing
   By, by, lully lullay!

DANCE OF THE SUGAR PLUM FAIRY

from THE NUTCRACKER

By PYOTR IL'YICH TCHAIKOVSKY

DING DONG! MERRILY ON HIGH!

French Carol

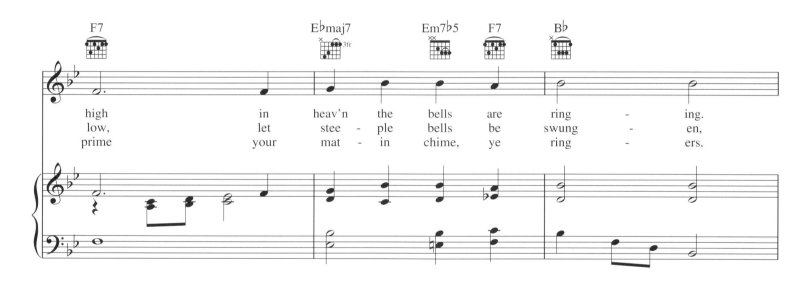

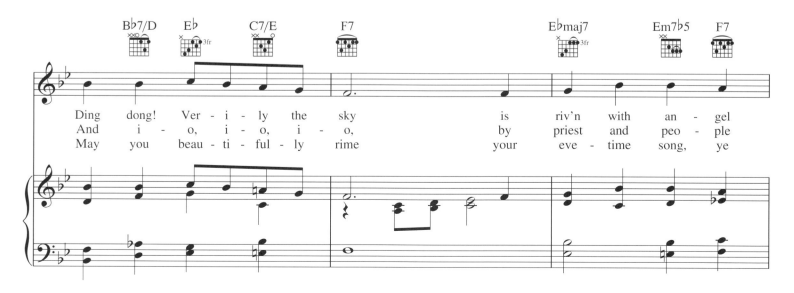

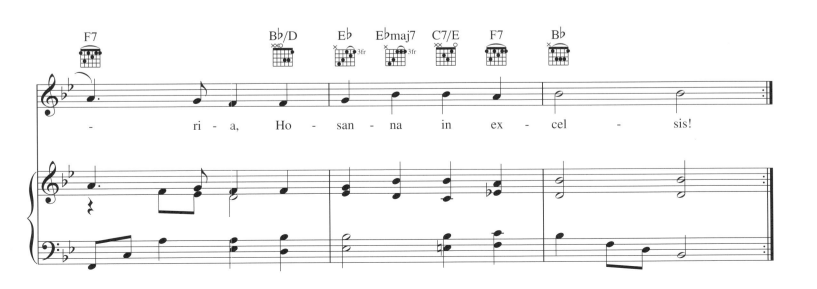

DO THEY KNOW IT'S CHRISTMAS?

Words and Music by M. URE
and B. GELDOF

FEELS LIKE CHRISTMAS

Words and Music by PAM WENDELL
and ELMO SHROPSHIRE

THE FIRST NOËL

17th Century English Carol
Music from W. Sandys' *Christmas Carols*

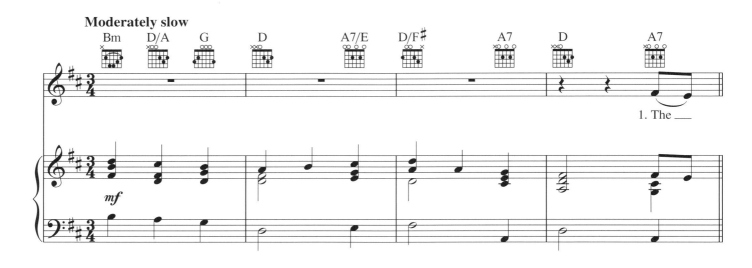

Moderately slow

1. The ___

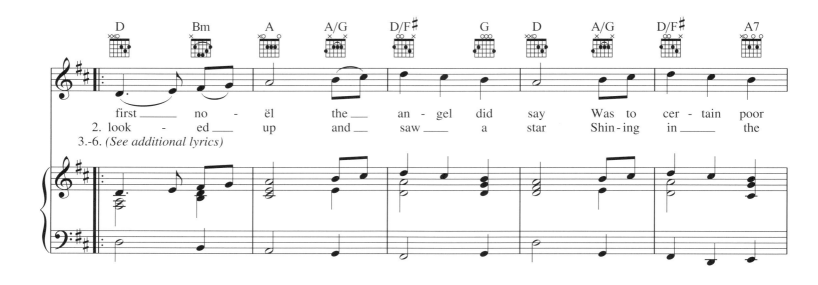

first ___ no - ël the ___ an - gel did say Was to cer - tain poor
2. look - ed ___ up and ___ saw a star Shin - ing in ___ the
3.-6. *(See additional lyrics)*

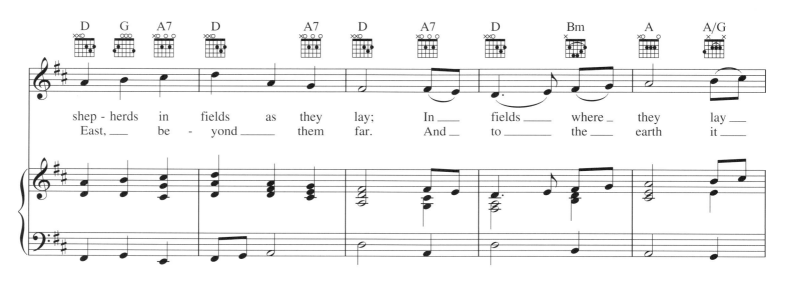

shep - herds in fields as they lay; In ___ fields ___ where ___ they lay ___
East, ___ be - yond ___ them far. And ___ to ___ the ___ earth it ___

Additional Lyrics

3. And by the light of that same star,
   Three wise men came from country far.
   To seek for a King was their intent,
   And to follow the star wherever it went.
   Refrain

4. This star drew nigh to the northwest;
   O'er Bethlehem it took its rest.
   And there it did both stop and stay,
   Right over the place where Jesus lay.
   Refrain

5. Then entered in those wise men three,
   Full rev'rently upon their knee;
   And offered there in His presence,
   Their gold and myrrh and frankincense.
   Refrain

6. Then let us all with one accord
   Sing praises to our heav'nly Lord,
   That hath made heav'n and earth of naught,
   And with His blood mankind hath bought.
   Refrain

FROSTY THE SNOW MAN

Words and Music by STEVE NELSON
and JACK ROLLINS

GOIN' ON A SLEIGHRIDE

Words and Music by
RALPH BLANE

GOD REST YE MERRY, GENTLEMEN

19th Century English Carol

GRANDMA GOT RUN OVER BY A REINDEER

Words and Music by
RANDY BROOKS

Grand-ma got run o - ver by a rein - deer walk-ing home from our house Christ-mas Eve. You can say there's no such thing as San - ta, but as for me and Grand-pa, we be-

88

You can say there's no such thing as San - ta, but as for me and Grand-pa, we be-

lieve.

Additional Lyrics

2. Now we're all so proud of Grandpa,
   He's been taking this so well.
   See him in there watching football,
   Drinking beer and playing cards with Cousin Mel.
   It's not Christmas without Grandma.
   All the family's dressed in black,
   And we just can't help but wonder:
   Should we open up her gifts or send them back?
   Chorus

3. Now the goose is on the table,
   And the pudding made of fig,
   And the blue and silver candles,
   That would just have matched the hair in Grandma's wig.
   I've warned all my friends and neighbors,
   Better watch out for yourselves.
   They should never give a license
   To a man who drives a sleigh and plays with elves.
   Chorus

GRANDMA'S KILLER FRUITCAKE

Words and Music by ELMO SHROPSHIRE
and RITA ABRAMS

Two-Beat Country Swing

The hol - i - days were up - on us and things were go - in' fine, 'til the day I heard the door - bell and a chill ran up my spine. I

GRANDPA'S GONNA SUE THE PANTS OFFA SANTA

Words and Music by RITA ABRAMS,
ELMO SHROPSHIRE and JON GAUGER

102

THE GREATEST GIFT OF ALL

Words and Music by
JOHN JARVIS

104

GREENWILLOW CHRISTMAS
from GREENWILLOW

By FRANK LOESSER

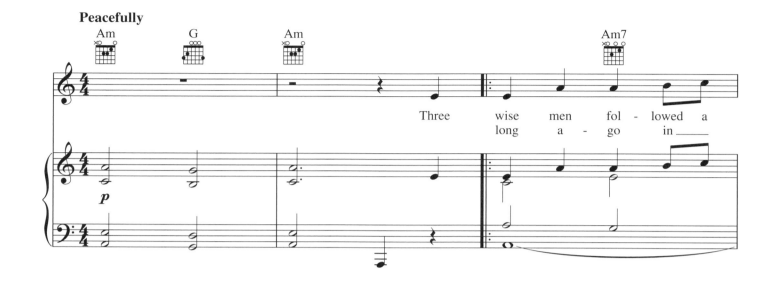

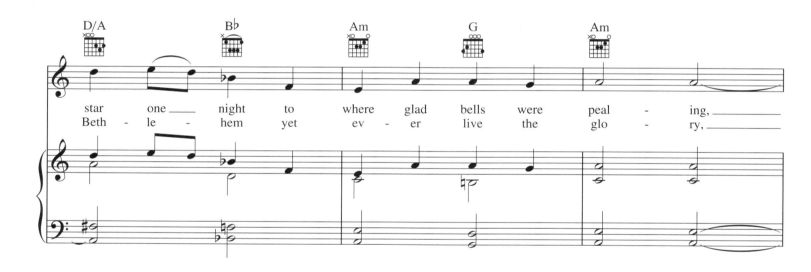

GROWN-UP CHRISTMAS LIST

Words and Music by DAVID FOSTER
and LINDA THOMPSON-JENNER

HALLELUJAH CHORUS
from MESSIAH

By GEORGE FRIDERIC HANDEL

HAPPY HOLIDAY

from the Motion Picture Irving Berlin's HOLIDAY INN

Words and Music by
IRVING BERLIN

Happy hol-i-day, _____ hap-py hol-i-day. _____ While the mer-ry bells keep ring-ing, may your ev-'ry wish come true. Hap-py

HAPPY NEW YEAR DARLING

Music and Lyrics by CARMEN LOMBARDO
and JOHNNY MARKS

Ev - 'ry time I hear "Auld Lang Syne," what mem - o - ries it brings!

Crowds that flow, pa - per horns that blow, and ev - 'ry - bod - y sings:

Hap - py New Year, Dar - ling! I give this toast to you.

HARD CANDY CHRISTMAS
from THE BEST LITTLE WHOREHOUSE IN TEXAS

Words and Music by
CAROL HALL

129

HARK! THE HERALD ANGELS SING

Words by CHARLES WESLEY
Altered by GEORGE WHITEFIELD
Music by FELIX MENDELSSOHN-BARTHOLDY
Arranged by WILLIAM H. CUMMINGS

Hark! The her - ald an - gels sing, _____
Christ, by high - est heav'n a - dored, _____
Hail, the heav'n - born Prince of Peace! _____

"Glo - ry to the new - born King! Peace on earth, and
Christ, the ev - er - last - ing Lord; Late in time be
Hail, the Sun of Right - eous - ness! Light and life to

mer - cy mild, _____ God and sin - ners rec - on - ciled."
hold Him come, _____ Off - spring of the vir - gin's womb.
all He brings, _____ Ris'n with heal - ing in His wings.

HERE COMES SANTA CLAUS
(Right Down Santa Claus Lane)

Words and Music by GENE AUTRY
and OAKLEY HALDEMAN

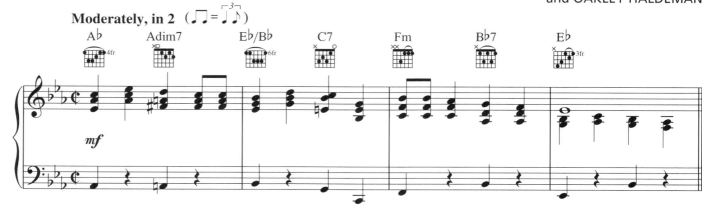

Here comes San-ta Claus! Here comes San-ta Claus! Right down San-ta Claus Lane!

Vix-en and Blitz-en and all his rein-deer are pull-ing on the rein.
He's got a bag that is filled with toys for the boys and girls a-gain.
He does-n't care if you're rich or poor, for he loves you just the same.
He'll come a-round when the chimes ring out; then it's Christ-mas morn a-gain.

Bells are ring-ing, chil-dren sing-ing, all is mer-ry and
Hear those sleigh-bells jin-gle jan-gle, what a beau-ti-ful
San-ta knows that we're God's chil-dren; that makes ev-'ry-thing
Peace on earth will come to all if we just fol-low the

bright.
sight.
right.   Hang your stock-ings and say your pray'rs,
light.   Jump in bed, cov-er up your head,   } 'cause
              Fill your hearts with a Christ-mas cheer,
              Let's give thanks to the Lord a-bove,

San-ta Claus comes to-night.   San-ta Claus comes to-night.

A HOLLY JOLLY CHRISTMAS

Music and Lyrics by
JOHNNY MARKS

Have a hol-ly jol-ly Christ-mas, it's the best time of the year.

I don't know if there'll be snow, but

have a cup of cheer. ___ Have a hol-ly jol-ly

(There's No Place Like)
HOME FOR THE HOLIDAYS

Words by AL STILLMAN
Music by ROBERT ALLEN

Moderately, with feeling

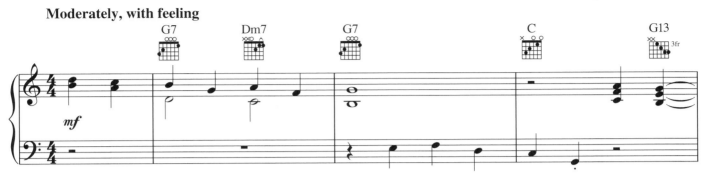

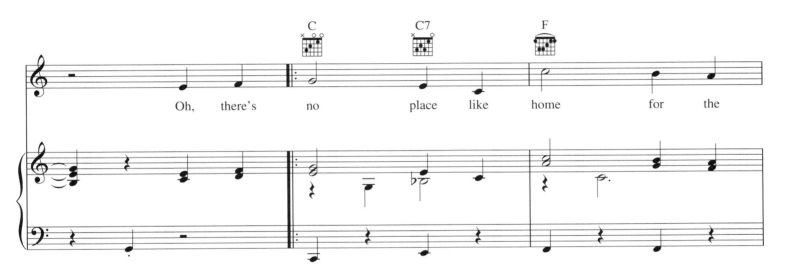

Oh, there's no place like home for the

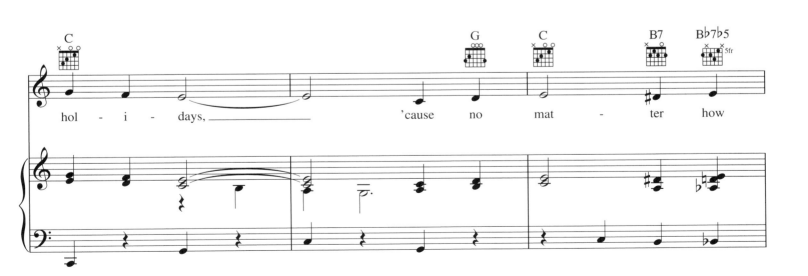

hol-i-days, ____ 'cause no mat-ter how

I HEARD THE BELLS ON CHRISTMAS DAY

Words by HENRY WADSWORTH LONGFELLOW
Adapted by JOHNNY MARKS
Music by JOHNNY MARKS

I STILL BELIEVE IN SANTA CLAUS

Words and Music by MAURICE STARR
and AL LANCELLOTTI

I WISH EVERYDAY COULD BE LIKE CHRISTMAS

Words and Music by DAVID ERWIN
and JIM CARTER

I'LL BE HOME FOR CHRISTMAS

Words and Music by KIM GANNON
and WALTER KENT

IT'S BEGINNING TO LOOK LIKE CHRISTMAS

By MEREDITH WILLSON

Moderately

It's be - gin - ning to look a lot like Christ - mas, ev - 'ry-where you go;

{ Take a
{ There's a

look in the five and ten, glis - ten - ing once a - gain, with
tree in the grand ho - tel, one in the park as well, with the

I'VE GOT MY LOVE TO KEEP ME WARM

from the 20th Century Fox Motion Picture ON THE AVENUE

Words and Music by
IRVING BERLIN

IT MUST HAVE BEEN THE MISTLETOE
(Our First Christmas)

By JUSTIN WILDE
and DOUG KONECKY

IT'S CHRISTMAS IN NEW YORK

Words and Music by
BILLY BUTT

JINGLE-BELL ROCK

Words and Music by JOE BEAL
and JIM BOOTHE

177

JINGLE BELLS

Words and Music by
J. PIERPONT

JINGLE, JINGLE, JINGLE

Music and Lyrics by
JOHNNY MARKS

Moderately, gaily

Jin - gle, jin - gle, jin - gle, you will

hear {my/his} sleigh - bells ring, {I am/Jol - ly} old Kris

Krin - gle, {I'm/is} the King of jin - gl - ing.

JOY TO THE WORLD

Words by ISAAC WATTS
Music by GEORGE FRIDERIC HANDEL
Arranged by LOWELL MASON

With spirit

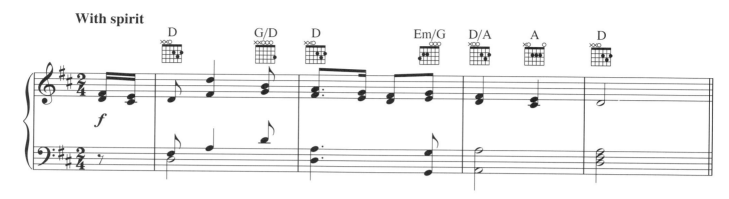

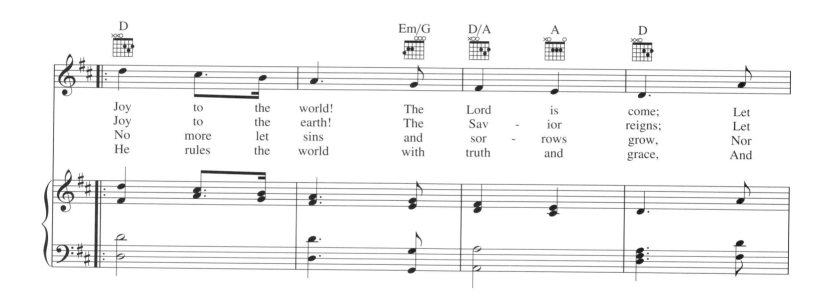

Joy to the world! The Lord is come; Let
Joy to the world! The earth! The Sav - ior reigns; Let
No more let sins and sor - rows grow, Nor
He rules the world with truth and grace, And

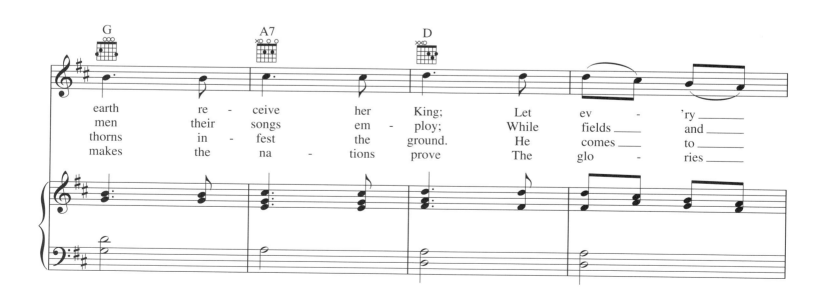

earth re - ceive her King; Let ev - 'ry _____
men their songs em - ploy; While fields _____ and _____
thorns in - fest the ground. He comes _____ to _____
makes the na - tions prove The glo - ries _____

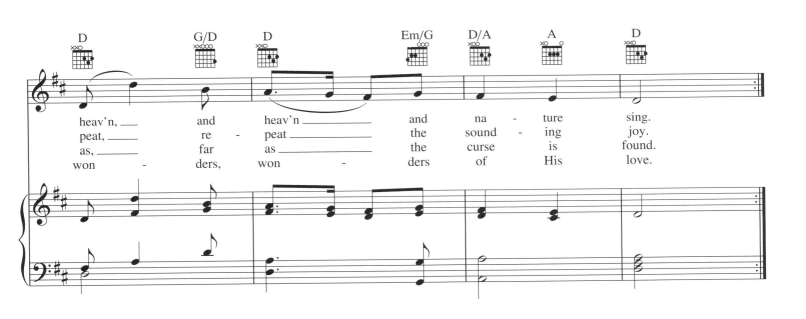

THE LAST MONTH OF THE YEAR
(What Month Was Jesus Born In?)

Words and Music by VERA HALL
Adapted and Arranged by RUBY PICKENS TARTT
and ALAN LOMAX

LET IT SNOW! LET IT SNOW! LET IT SNOW!

Words by SAMMY CAHN
Music by JULE STYNE

Moderately

Oh, the weath-er out-side is fright-ful, but the

fire is so de-light-ful, and since we've no place to go, Let it

snow! Let it snow! Let it snow! It does-n't show signs of stop-ping, and I
fi-re is slow-ly dy-ing and, my

LITTLE SAINT NICK

Words and Music by BRIAN WILSON
and MIKE LOVE

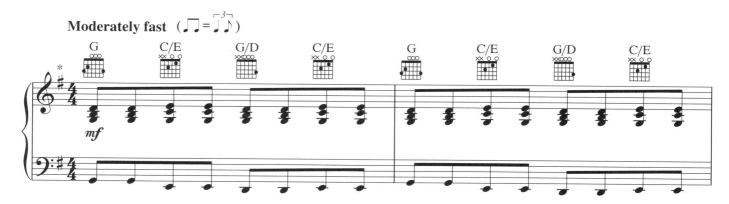

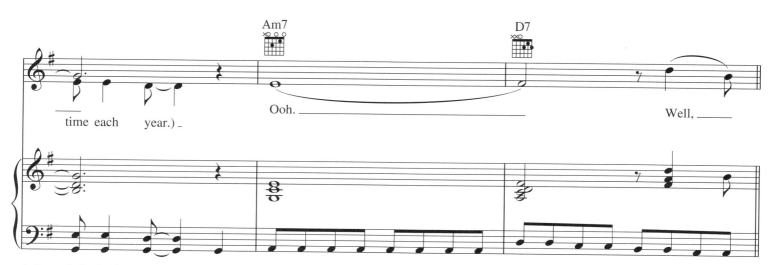

* *Recorded a half step lower.*

way up north where the air gets cold, ___ there's a
lit - tle bob - sled, we call it Old Saint Nick, ___ but she'll
haul - in' through the snow at a fright - 'nin' speed ___ with a

tale a - bout Chirst - mas that you've all been told. ___ And a
walk a to - bog - gan with a four - speed stick. ___ She's
half a doz - en deer ___ with ___ Ru - dy to lead. He's

real fa - mous cat all dressed up in red, ___ and he
can - dy ap - ple red with a ski for a wheel, and when
got - ta wear his gog - gles 'cause the snow real - ly flies, and he's

MARCH OF THE TOYS
from BABES IN TOYLAND

By VICTOR HERBERT

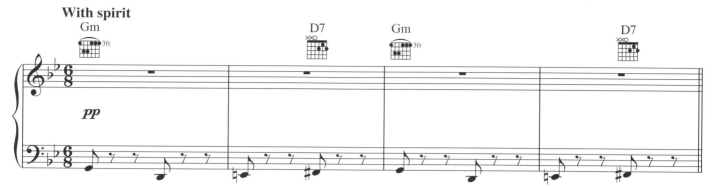

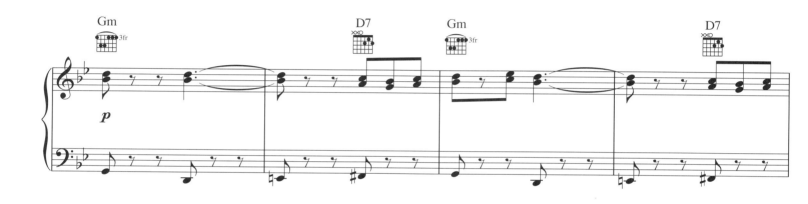

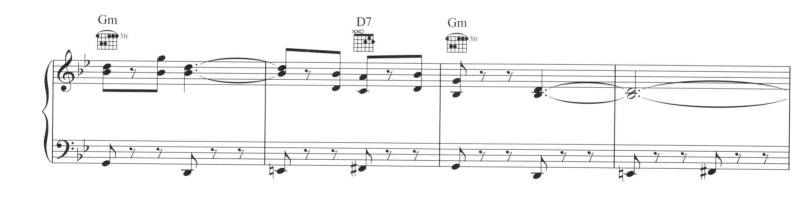

A MARSHMALLOW WORLD

Words by CARL SIGMAN
Music by PETER DE ROSE

MARY'S LITTLE BOY CHILD

Words and Music by
JESTER HAIRSTON

MELE KALIKIMAKA

Words and Music by
R. ALEX ANDERSON

Lyrics:

"Jin - gle Bells" up - on a steel gui - tar;

through the palms we see the same bright star.

Me - le Ka - li - ki - ma - ka is the thing to say _____ on a

MERRY CHRISTMAS, DARLING

Words and Music by RICHARD CARPENTER
and FRANK POOLER

THE MERRY CHRISTMAS POLKA

Words by PAUL FRANCIS WEBSTER
Music by SONNY BURKE

Moderate Polka tempo

tun - ing up the fid - dles now, the fid - dles now, the fid - dles now. There's

wine to warm the mid - dles now and set your head a - whirl. A-

214

216

THE NIGHT BEFORE CHRISTMAS SONG

Music by JOHNNY MARKS
Lyrics adapted by JOHNNY MARKS
from CLEMENT MOORE'S Poem

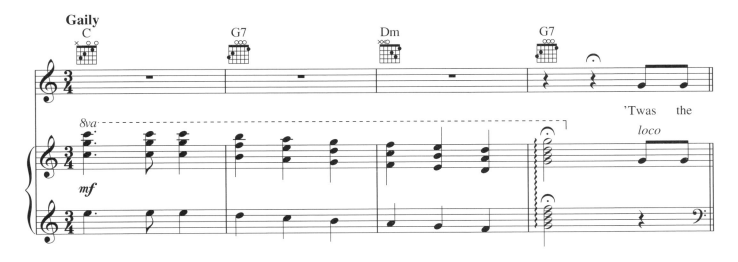

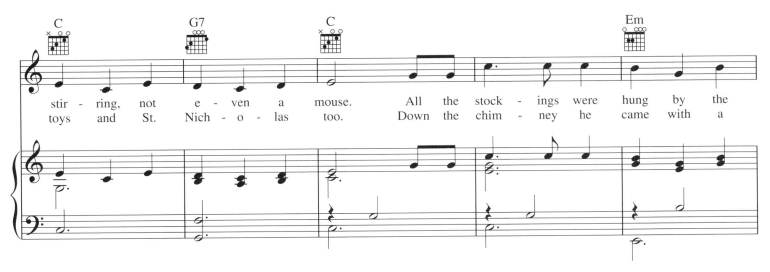

MISTLETOE AND HOLLY

Words and Music by FRANK SINATRA,
DOK STANFORD and HENRY W. SANICOLA

Medium Bounce

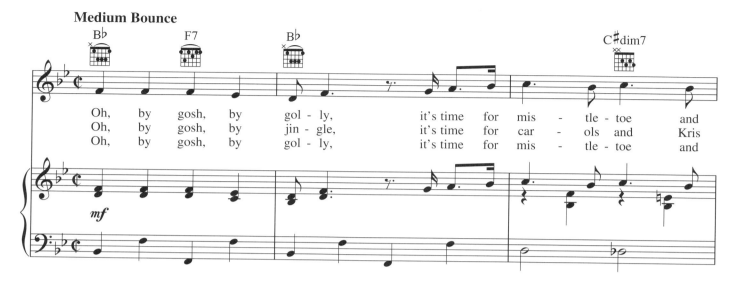

Oh, by gosh, by gol-ly, it's time for mis-tle-toe and
Oh, by gosh, by jin-gle, it's time for car-ols and Kris
Oh, by gosh, by gol-ly, it's time for mis-tle-toe and

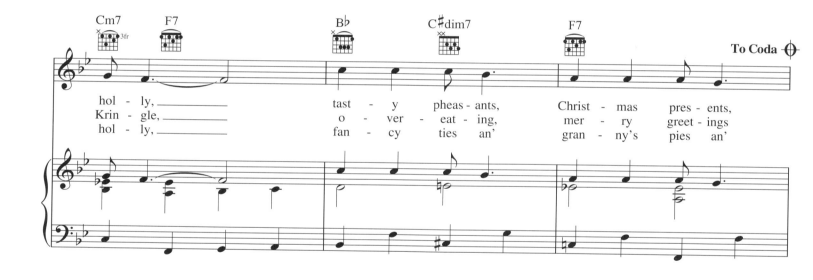

hol-ly,_____ tast-y pheas-ants, Christ-mas pres-ents,
Krin-gle,_____ o-ver-eat-ing, mer-ry greet-ings
hol-ly,_____ fan-cy ties an' gran-ny's pies an'

To Coda ⊕

coun-try-sides cov-ered with snow.
from ___ rel-a-tives you don't know.

THE MOST WONDERFUL TIME OF THE YEAR

Words and Music by EDDIE POLA
and GEORGE WYLE

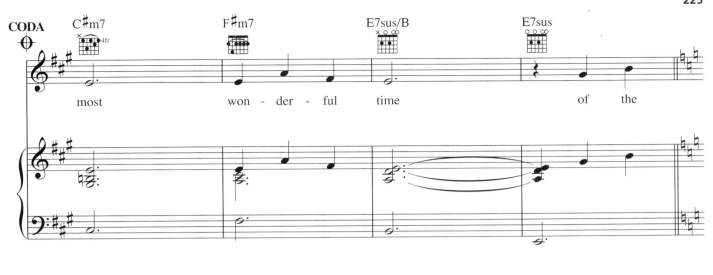

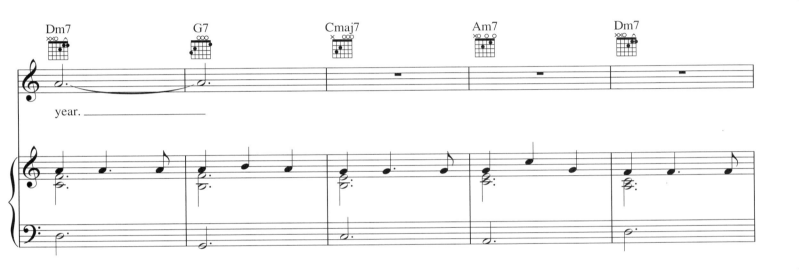

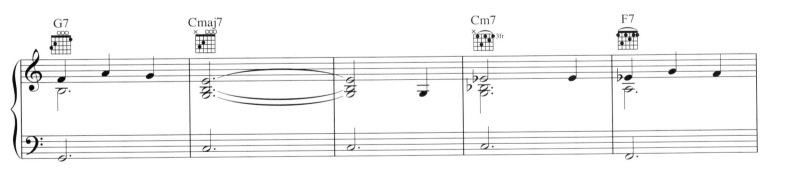

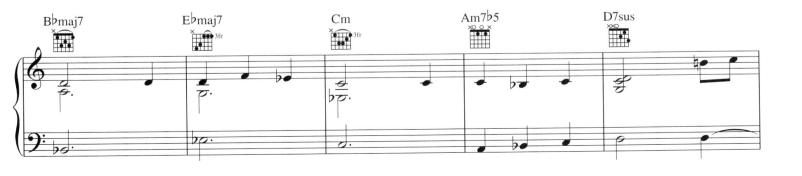

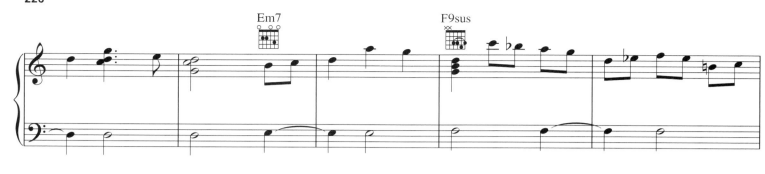

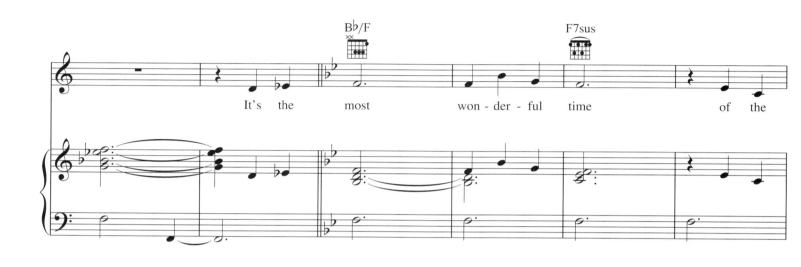

It's the most won-der-ful time of the

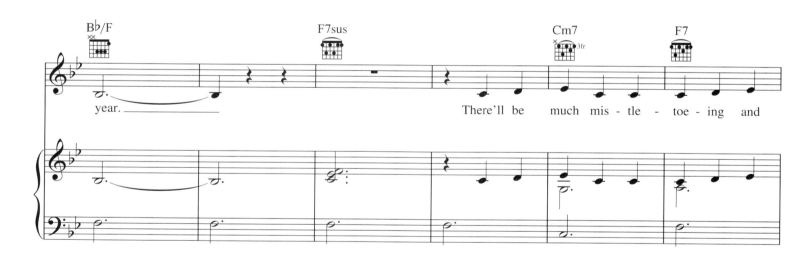

year. _____ There'll be much mis-tle-toe-ing and

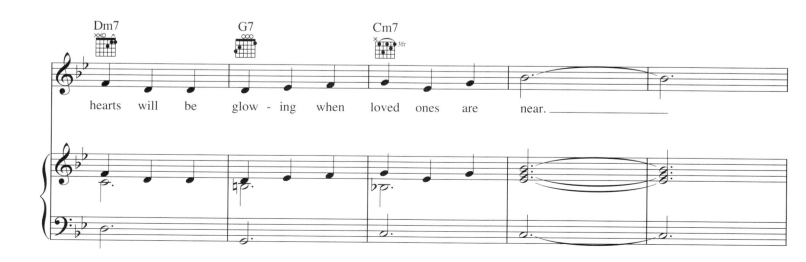

hearts will be glow-ing when loved ones are near. _____

MY ONLY WISH THIS YEAR

Words and Music by BRIAN KIERULF
and JOSHUA SCHWARTZ

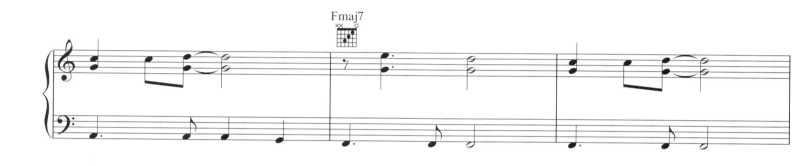

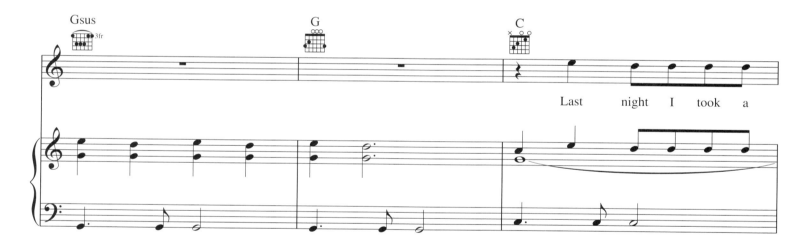

Last night I took a

walk in the snow. ___ Cou- ples hold- ing hands; plac- es to go. ___

NUTTIN' FOR CHRISTMAS

Words and Music by ROY BENNETT
and SID TEPPER

Brightly

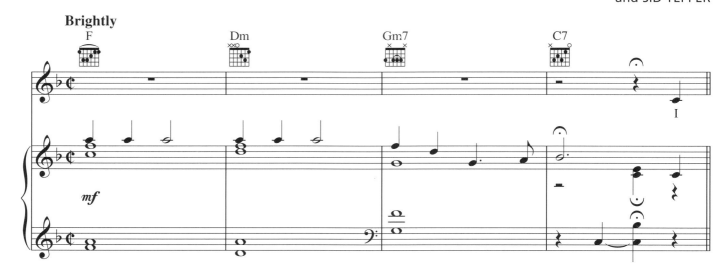

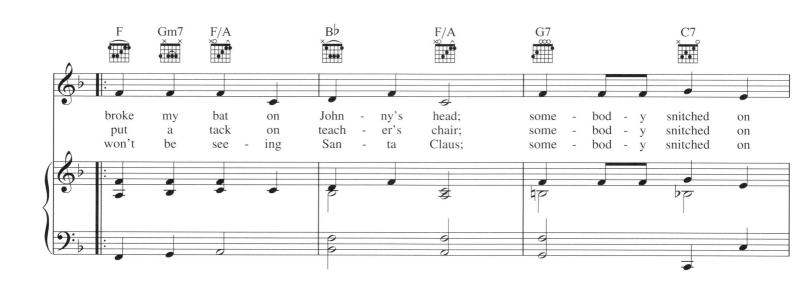

broke my bat on John - ny's head; some - bod - y snitched on
put a tack on teach - er's chair; some - bod - y snitched on
won't be see - ing San - ta Claus; some - bod - y snitched on

me. I hid a frog in sis - ter's bed;
me. I tied a knot in Su - sie's hair;
me. He won't come vis - it me be - cause

O CHRISTMAS TREE

Traditional German Carol

243

O COME, ALL YE FAITHFUL
(Adeste fideles)

Music by JOHN FRANCIS WADE
Latin Words translated by FREDERICK OAKELEY

O HOLY NIGHT

French Words by PLACIDE CAPPEAU
English Words by JOHN S. DWIGHT
Music by ADOLPHE ADAM

O LITTLE TOWN OF BETHLEHEM

Words by PHILLIPS BROOKS
Music by LEWIS H. REDNER

1. O lit - tle town of Beth - le - hem, How
2. Christ is born of Mar - y, And
3.,4. *(See additional lyrics)*

still we _____ see thee lie! A - bove thy deep and
gath - ered _____ all a - bove, While mor - tals sleep and the

dream - less sleep The si - lent _____ stars go by. Yet
an - gels sleep keep Their watch of _____ won - d'ring love. O

Additional Lyrics

3. How silently, how silently
   The wondrous Gift is giv'n!
   So God imparts to human hearts
   The blessings of His heav'n.
   No ear may hear His coming,
   But in this world of sin,
   Where meek souls will receive Him still,
   The dear Christ enters in.

4. O Holy Child of Bethlehem,
   Descend to us, we pray.
   Cast out our sin, and enter in,
   Be born in us today.
   We hear the Christmas angels
   The great glad tidings tell.
   O come to us, abide with us,
   Our Lord Immanuel!

AN OLD FASHIONED CHRISTMAS

Music and Lyrics by
JOHNNY MARKS

OLD TOY TRAINS

Words and Music by
ROGER MILLER

PARADE OF THE WOODEN SOLDIERS

English Lyrics by BALLARD MacDONALD
Music by LEON JESSEL

PRECIOUS PROMISE

Words and Music by
STEVEN CURTIS CHAPMAN

Oh, what a pre - cious prom - ise, oh, what a gift __ of love; __

an an - gel tells __ a vir - gin that __

the an - gel told them. _____

A

star's light ___ fills up ___ the dark sky ___

as the night of pre - cious prom - ise is un -

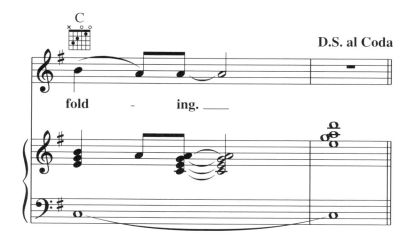

fold - ing. ___

D.S. al Coda

CODA

man - ger in Beth - le - hem. _____

PRETTY PAPER

Words and Music by
WILLIE NELSON

ROCKIN' AROUND THE CHRISTMAS TREE

Music and Lyrics by
JOHNNY MARKS

Moderate Shuffle

Rock-in' a-round the Christ-mas tree ___ at the Christ-mas par-ty hop. ___

Mis-tle-toe hung where you can see ___ ev-'ry

cou-ple tries to stop. Rock-in' a-round the

RUDOLPH THE RED-NOSED REINDEER

Music and Lyrics by
JOHNNY MARKS

SANTA BABY

By JOAN JAVITS,
PHIL SPRINGER and TONY SPRINGER

Mis - ter "Claus," I feel as though I know ya, _____ so

you won't mind if I should get fa - mil - ya, will ya?

San - ta Ba - by, just slip a sa - ble un - der the tree ___
San - ta Ba - by, one lit - tle thing I real - ly do need; ___

SANTA CLAUS IS COMIN' TO TOWN

Words by HAVEN GILLESPIE
Music by J. FRED COOTS

You bet-ter watch out, you bet-ter not cry, bet-ter not pout, I'm tell-ing you why:

San-ta Claus is com-in' to town.

He's

SHAKE ME I RATTLE
(Squeeze Me I Cry)

Words and Music by HAL HACKADY
and CHARLES NAYLOR

SILENT NIGHT

Words by JOSEPH MOHR
Translated by JOHN F. YOUNG
Music by FRANZ X. GRUBER

SILVER BELLS
from the Paramount Picture THE LEMON DROP KID

Words and Music by JAY LIVINGSTON
and RAY EVANS

Eb

Eb6

F7

smile af - ter smile, and on ev - 'ry street cor - ner you
San - ta's big scene, and a - bove all this bus - tle you

Bb

hear: _____
hear: _____

Sil - ver bells, _____

Eb

F

C7

sil - ver bells, _____ it's Christ - mas -

F7

Bb

time in the cit - y. _____

SING WE NOW OF CHRISTMAS
(Noël nouvelet)

Traditional French Carol

Joyfully

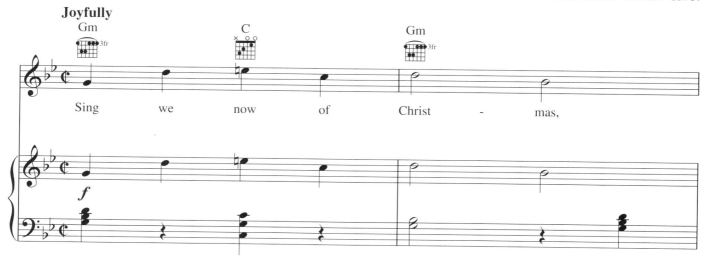

Sing we now of Christ - mas,

No - ël ___ sing we here. Sing our grate - ful

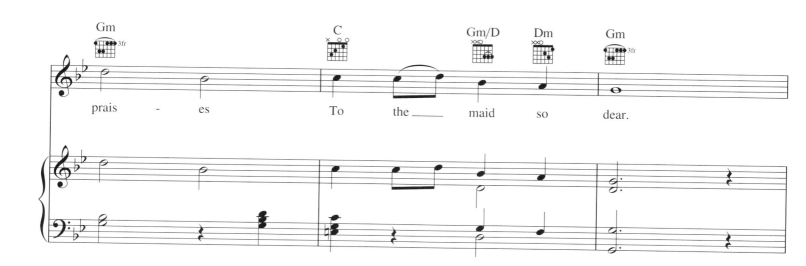

prais - es To the ___ maid so dear.

SNOWFALL

Lyrics by RUTH THORNHILL
Music by CLAUDE THORNHILL

SOMEWHERE IN MY MEMORY

from the Twentieth Century Fox Motion Picture HOME ALONE

Words by LESLIE BRICUSSE
Music by JOHN WILLIAMS

SUZY SNOWFLAKE

Words and Music by SID TEPPER
and ROY BENNETT

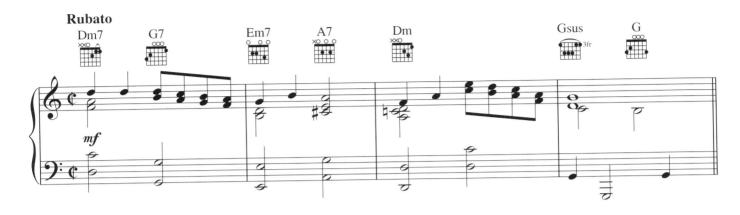

Here comes Su - zy Snow - flake, dressed in a snow - white
Here comes Su - zy Snow - flake, soon you will hear her

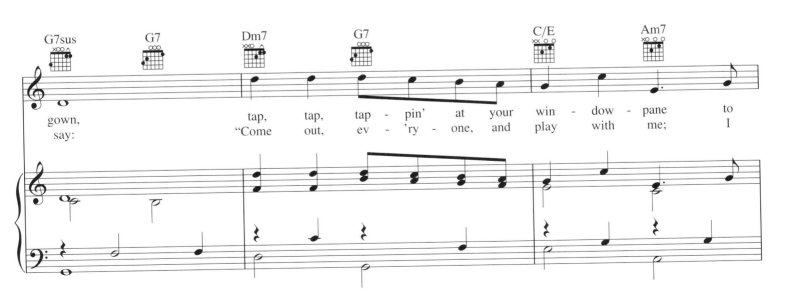

gown,
say: "Come tap out, ev - 'ry - one, and play with me; I
tap, tap, tap - pin' at your win - dow - pane to

STILL, STILL, STILL

Salzburg Melody, c.1819
Traditional Austrian Text

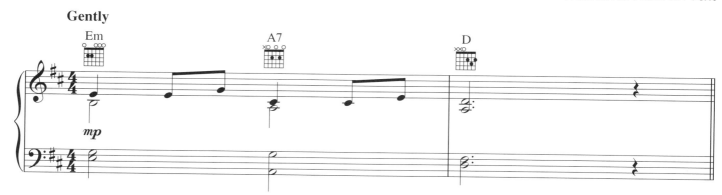

Still, _____ still, _____ still; _____ to _____ sleep is _____ now His _____
Sleep, _____ sleep, _____ sleep, while _____ we Thy _____ vig - il _____

will. On Mar - y's _____ breast He rests in _____ slum - ber
keep. And an - gels _____ come He from Heav - en _____ sing - ing

TENNESSEE CHRISTMAS

Words and Music by AMY GRANT
and GARY CHAPMAN

Come on weath - er - man _____ give us _____ a fore -
Ev - 'ry now _____ and then _____ I get _____ a wan -

- cast snow - y white. _____
- derin' urge _____ to see,

Can't you hear _____ the prayers _____ of ev - 'ry child -
may - be Cal - i - for - nia, may - be Tin -

TOYLAND

Words by GLEN MacDONOUGH
Music by VICTOR HERBERT

Very slow and dreamily

When you've grown up, my dears, _____ and there
you've grown up, my dears, _____ the

are as old as I, _____ you'll of-ten pon-der
comes a drea-ry day _____ when 'mid the locks of

on the years that roll so swift-ly by, my dears, that
black ap-pears that the first pale gleam of gray, my dears, that the

THIS ONE'S FOR THE CHILDREN

Words and Music by
MAURICE STARR

'TWAS THE NIGHT BEFORE CHRISTMAS

Words by CLEMENT CLARK MOORE
Music by F. HENRI KLICKMAN

Additional Lyrics

3. With a little old driver so lively and quick,
   I knew in a moment it must be St. Nick.
   More rapid than eagles his coursers they came,
   And he whistled, and shouted, and called them by name:
   "Now, Dasher! Now, Dancer! Now, Prancer! Now, Vixen!
   On, Comet! On, Cupid! On, Donder and Blitzen!
   To the top of the porch, to the top of the wall!
   Now dash away, dash away, dash away all!"

4. As dry leaves that before the wild hurricane fly,
   When they meet with an obstacle, mount to the sky,
   So up to the house-top the coursers they flew,
   With the sleigh full of toys, and St. Nicholas, too.
   And then in a twinkling I heard on the roof
   The prancing and pawing of each little hoof.
   As I drew in my head, and was turning around,
   Down the chimney St. Nicholas came with a bound.

5. He was dressed all in fur from his head to his foot,
   And his clothes were all tarnished with ashes and soot;
   A bundle of toys he had flung on his back,
   And he looked like a peddler just opening his pack.
   His eyes how they twinkled! His dimples how merry!
   His cheeks were like roses, his nose like a cherry.
   His droll little mouth was drawn up like a bow,
   And the beard of his chin was as white as the snow.

6. The stump of a pipe he held tight in his teeth,
   And the smoke, it encircled his head like a wreath.
   He had a broad face, and a round little belly
   That shook, when he laughed, like a bowl full of jelly.
   He was chubby and plump, a right jolly old elf,
   And I laughed when I saw him, in spite of myself.
   A wink of his eye, and a twist of his head,
   Soon gave me to know I had nothing to dread.

7. He spoke not a word, but went straight to his work,
   And filled all the stockings; then turned with a jerk,
   And laying his finger aside of his nose,
   And giving a nod, up the chimney he rose.
   He sprang to his sleigh, to his team gave a whistle,
   And away they all fled like the down of a thistle;
   But I heard him exclaim, ere he drove out of sight:
   "Happy Christmas to all, and to all a Good-night!"

WE NEED A LITTLE CHRISTMAS

from MAME

Music and Lyric by
JERRY HERMAN

UP ON THE HOUSETOP

Words and Music by
B.R. HANBY

WE THREE KINGS OF ORIENT ARE

Words and Music by
JOHN H. HOPKINS, JR.

We three kings of O - ri - ent are; Bear - ing gifts we tra - verse a - far, Field and foun - tain, moor and moun - tain, Fol - low - ing yon - der

WE WISH YOU A MERRY CHRISTMAS

Traditional English Folksong

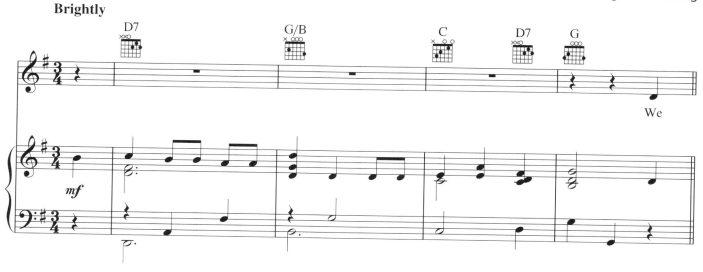

We

wish you a mer-ry Christ-mas, We wish you a mer-ry Christ-mas, We

wish you a mer-ry Christ-mas, and a hap-py New Year. Good

WHAT ARE YOU DOING NEW YEAR'S EVE?

By FRANK LOESSER

WHAT CHILD IS THIS?

Words by WILLIAM C. DIX
16th Century English Melody

WHEN SANTA CLAUS GETS YOUR LETTER

Music and Lyrics by
JOHNNY MARKS

THE WHITE WORLD OF WINTER

Words by MITCHELL PARISH
Music by HOAGY CARMICHAEL

YOU'RE ALL I WANT FOR CHRISTMAS

Words and Music by GLEN MOORE
and SEGER ELLIS